My Heritage
Treasuring Our Treasures

Pastor Irma Jean Holland

Copyright 2016 by Pastor Irma Jean Holland.

All rights reserved.
Printed in the United States of America.

No portion of this book may be reproduced, stored in a retrieval system, or transmitted in any form or by any means—electronic, mechanical, photocopy, recording, scanning, or other—except for brief quotations in critical reviews or articles, without the prior written permission of the publisher.

Unless otherwise noted, Scripture quotations are taken from The Holy Bible, King James Version.

ISBN 978-1-943650-39-2

Library of Congress Number 2016959650

Published 2016 by **BookCrafters**
Parker, Colorado.
www.bookcrafters.net

Cover design by Wiley Smith.

This book may be purchased at online bookstores.

Table of Contents

Foreword..1
    Pastor Max Smith
Acknowledgements...5
    Dr. Jean Holland
Preface...7
    Dr. Jean Holland
Dedication..11
    Sandra Coolman: A City Set on a Hill
Parker Memories...15
    Jeanette Ford
I'm Counting on You...22
    Casey Johnese
My ("Space") Story...33
    Josh Palmer
The Lady…Jean Holland..42
    VaLynn Mills
Light of God..48
    Elizabeth Loper
Honor Christ in Your Service.....................................54
    Lisa Blaine
My Greatest Influences...60
    Camille Gordon
The One Who Does the Work Gets the Blessing.....67
    Vicky Keller
In the Beginning...74
    Dee Wells

Bloom Where You Are Planted..................................79
    Bobbie Lively

Foreword

Treasuring Our Treasures

I came to Jesus Name Tabernacle as a 16 year old man, in 1986. After one visit, I was hooked on this wonderful "Pentecostal" experience. During this time, I was a junior in High School at Richland Attendance Center. I went to school with several of the young adults from my church, including some classes with my future wife. I was a good young man but still searching for something deeper in the Spirit. In 1987, I received the baptism of the Holy Ghost, with the evidence of speaking in tongues, as the Spirit gave the utterance. I was never the same after this. My life at Jesus Name Tabernacle was lived under subjection to my pastor, Dr. Jean Holland. Skipping forward, I have been under her training in ministry for over 30 years.

   The simple definition of "Heritage" is "the traditions, achievements, beliefs, etc., that are part of the history of a person." In the depths of my heart and mind I value the treasure of having known and been shepherded by someone such as Dr. Irma Jean Holland, Senior Pastor Emeritus of Jesus

Name Tabernacle. She has pastored over 30 years in Florence MS and celebrated her 80th birthday in this year of 2016.

My wife and I have served as youth pastors at JNT. The instruction and example we have been privileged to; as we worked alongside Pastor Holland, has developed our ministry in teaching, preaching, music, and outreach. The results we have witnessed firsthand and many are expressed in the stories recorded in this book and the previous, "My Heritage" books

This third book in the series, "My Heritage Treasuring Treasures," continues to share the tremendous miraculous testimonies of those who have been blessed by Dr. Holland's dedication to the Lord and to His church. Her parents, Wiley and Eula Holland, contributed with prayer, fasting, and godly living to the great harvest that is portrayed in each book.

1 Corinthians 3:6 I have planted, Apollos watered; but God gave the increase.

As I write this foreword my spirit is full to overflowing. I love Senior Pastor Holland and I love JNT Church. She always saw something in me that I did not see and I give her honor for that. On June 12, 2016, Pastor Holland chose to place me as pastor of Jesus Name Tabernacle. She placed the mantle upon me as the Lord led her to do so. By the grace and mercy of our Lord and Savior Jesus Christ we will continue to work the great harvest. We have been experiencing growth and revival services at our church, and are excited about an unlimited future ahead as we advance the kingdom "In Jesus."

Rev. Max Smith,
Pastor of Jesus Name Tabernacle

Acknowledgements

Third book: Treasuring Our Treasures

I would need an entire book to express my gratitude to the Lord for placing treasures all through my life. Treasures of friends and family that I cherish dearly.

My family, and my church family, my minister and pastor friends and those mentioned in this and the previous two books share my heritage

It has been my privilege to serve the Lord with "Gladness."

> "The Lord is good and His mercy is everlasting and His truth endures to all generations." Psalm 100

Again, I acknowledge family and friends who have made this book possible. Each testimony expresses the beautiful process of the grace of God in our lives.

Revelation 12:11a And they overcame him by the blood of the lamb; and by the word of their testimony."

Jesus Name Tabernacle church family, I love you. Thank you Pastor Max Smith and your godly wife Sister Peggy Smith and her mother, Sister Nancy Howell. Your devotion to the work of the Lord is and has always been a beautiful example.

I acknowledge the work not only in this book, Treasuring Our Treasures, but those who work in children's church, outreach, prayer meetings, bookstore and so much more.

Thank you,

Dr. Irma Jean Holland
Senior Pastor Emeritus

Preface

I am privileged to experience the beautiful blessings of God at Jesus Name Tabernacle. I am now eighty years of age and enjoying each generation as they step up to the plate and eagerly consecrate their lives to the call of God.

The testimonies in this book will be a blessing to everyone. We can claim the promises the Lord repeatedly gives to us. *Act 2:39 For the promise is unto you, and to your children and to all that are afar off, even as many as the Lord our God shall call.*

Looking back over the years of my life; I am keenly aware of how God has surrounded me with people to help in my ministry. Many of my family and close friends have gone on to be with the Lord but they will never be forgotten. Jesus Name Tabernacle was and is blessed with gifted musicians, teachers, workers, outreach, and fundraisers teams. More than any Pastor could hope for.

At the beginning of 2016 the Lord began to speak to my heart that it was His time for me to rest and pass the mantle to someone else. There wasn't any struggle or doubt as to who it would be. It was the perfect will of God for it to be Reverend Max Smith. He is and always has been one of the most fervent and dedicated ministers in the church. He and his wife, Sister Peggy, and their sons, love the church. Visiting the sick, mowing the acreage, music programs, youth leaders and much more is the total design for their lives.

Rev. Max has, for many years, totally dedicated himself to serving and ministering to others. His many talents and gifts served to make my work lighter especially during my times of sickness. From the beginning of my calling to pastor and actually for all of my life I have known that the call to pastor is a call to feed the sheep of God's pasture.

God manifested His presence so beautifully during the ordination service. Love flowed from the throne of God and through the hearts of His people. I reflected on the providence of God. The Lord had planned my path and prepared us for this day. I was reminded of God's incredible faithfulness.

We are nearing the coming of the Lord and we do not know what we will face. Church, let's keep our lamps trimmed and burning bright. *"Behold the bridegroom cometh."*

2 Timothy 4:2 Preach the Word: be instant in season, out of season; reprove, rebuke, exhort with all longsuffering and doctrine.

2 Chronicles 7:14 If my people which are called by my name, shall humble themselves, and pray, and seek my face, and turn from their wicked ways; then will I hear from heaven, and will forgive their sin, and will heal their land.

Dr. Irma Jean Holland
Senior Pastor Emeritus

Dedication

This book is dedicated to Sandra Coolman — A CITY SET ON A HILL

Matthew 5:14 "Ye are the light of the world. A city that is set on an hill cannot be hid"

In these few words Jesus gave a word picture referring to those that follow him and are filled with His Spirit are the "Light of the World."

In the month of February 2016 just such a light and city was manifested in Florence, MS in the life and family of Sandra Coolman and Barney Coolman. They had been married 50 years and lived for God most of their life. To help celebrate their anniversary their family and friends along with their church family met at a local restaurant.

In a world of darkness and confusion a family such as the Coolman family stands out for the world to see what Jesus can and will do if He is the center of their life. The many stories the family and friends share about the elder Coolman's prove the above to be true. With great integrity they lived as Godly examples for their children, grandchildren and in fact everyone.

This family magnifies and brings to light how the Lord has blessed and used them and their family for His glory. Sis. Cheryl Coolman wrote a beautiful chapter in "My Heritage Giving to the Lord." The chapter is named "Love Unfolded." Several pictures of the family are included also.

The following Sunday after the 50th wedding anniversary celebration most of the family including those traveling from out of town came to service at Jesus Name Tabernacle for the evening service. Sister Coolman showed great courage and strength even though battling sickness and had been diagnosed with cancer. Two of her sons, Daniel and Steve preached a double header.

The early lives of Brother and Sister Coolman are beautiful. They built their lives on "the Rock Christ Jesus" therefore they make up "A City Set on A Hill."

Homegoing Service
for
Sis. Sandra Cortrella Coolman
January 22, 1948 ~ September 14, 2016

You will probably read in your local newspaper that Sandra Contrella Coolman has passed away—Don't believe a word of it! At this moment she is more alive than ever before. She has gone up higher, that's all. Out of this old house of clay into a house that is immortal. A body that cannot feel pain, that sin cannot taint, a body fashioned unto His glorious body.

Sis. Coolman lived in Richland, MS for 20 years and was a member of Jesus Name Tabernacle. She worked as a CNA with Oxford Home Health after retiring from Wal-Mart as a sales associate. She was a very loving wife, mother, and active church member.

Left to cherish her memory is her loving husband of 50 years, Barney Coolman of Pearl, sons, Steve (Kandy) Coolman of Richland, Daniel (Cheryl) of Pearl, Jesse (Sabrina) Coolman of Florence; daughter, Becky (Chauncey) Fonville of Brandon; brother, Earnest (Laura) LeMoine of Conroe, TX;

sisters, Francis Fisher of Hargis, LA and Elaine (Mike) Starovic of Conroe, TX; Grandchildren, Austin, Micah, Tucker, Julea, Ethan Todd Coolman and Amber and Isabel Fonville, and the Jesus Name Tabernacle Church family and a host of friends.

Parker Memories of Vidalia Faith Tabernacle Pentecostal Church

By Jeanette Ford

The first time I can remember the Hollands; we were living in Wisner, LA. Bro. Wiley Holland and his daughter, Sis. Jean, (maybe more) came to our church at Kendricks Ferry. I remember Sis. Jean Holland standing so tall and regal playing that big bass fiddle and Bro. Holland preaching; "Dearly Beloved!" I don't remember his sermon, but I remember how sweet and gentle he was. This was in about the year of 1957. I believe J.E. and Irene Parker were going to his church in Vidalia. During this time, Sis. Peggy Richards and Sis. Mickey Eaton were holding a tent revival. My daddy, Jesse Parker, and his brother, Buck Parker, got the Holy Ghost at this revival. Sis. Jean Holland would come visit us in Wisner. She would bring her reel to reel movie machine and show us movies she had recorded. I remember she had one cartoon that was very funny about skunks trying to cross a road. We kids really liked that.

During Thanksgiving holiday in 1959, Daddy moved us to Vidalia, Louisiana. We all loved the move. I became friends with Doris Guy. We were the best of friends—still are. I would stay at her house a lot. If I wasn't at her house then she was at mine. I remember Bro. George Guy and little Bro. Jerry Holland picking at us all the time and trying to make us holler. Aunt Sarah Guy would say in her sweet soft voice, "Now boys! Go outside and leave these girls alone!"

I was only 12 years old when we made the move; you had to be 13 years old to go into the Senior Young People's Sunday School Class. I was turning 13 in December so Uncle Charles Guy let me go into the Senior Class. I was in his Sunday School class only a few short weeks when he made me the Treasurer of our class. I was so proud of that.

Many times I would go home with Doris after Sunday School. We would go to Bro. and Sis. Holland's for dinner. Sis. Eula Holland's table would be so full of all her delicious foods that she prepared before church time. She would make a huge chocolate cake. My goodness! If you never ate her chocolate cake you really missed something. It must have had 6 or 8 layers of fluffy yellow cake with her chocolate icing in between each layer—on top and all the sides. There are no words to describe that cake. After we all ate dinner, Bro. Holland would stretch out on the sofa to rest. I can remember seeing him lying there with one hand raised like he was praying—He probably was.

I remember times when Bro. Wiley Holland's brother, Bro. Matt Holland, would be visiting. They would be fasting. They both would sit at both ends of Sis. Eula Holland's big table that was loaded with food, and after the blessing was prayed, they both would turn their empty water glasses upside down on their plates. They would sit with everyone and talk. I couldn't see back then, at the age of 13, how they could sit there and not eat that delicious food. I understand it now. When the Goodman's would visit, Bro. Howard Goodman would go to the living room after eating one of Sis. Holland's meals, and would say, "Okay, Lord; I'm suffering in comfort."

I was always fascinated by that big old drum at the church. Sis. Jean Holland told Arlene, my sister, to teach me how to play it. I loved that thing! I still do! It wasn't long before I was playing in church. That was my joy! Bro. Holland bought a new lighter weight tambourine just so I could play better. I loved that drum! My sisters and I used to sing together. I guess our signature song was, "Goodbye World, Goodbye." We still sing it when we all get together.

I remember the first instant miracle that I actually witnessed. Daddy, mama, my three younger sisters, along with Bro. Holland and I had gone to a fellowship meeting at Kendricks Ferry. We were coming home after church when my sister, Leah, began to have one of her seizures. Daddy stopped the car and he and Bro. Holland got out and went behind the station wagon. Bro. Holland said in a firm voice, "Bro. Parker, this is enough of this!" They laid hands on her and prayed. She went back to sleep and never has had another seizure.

I can remember when Sis. Jean and Sis. Arlene, my sister, began evangelizing. We hated for them to be gone so long. Once they were out in Mississippi, and Daddy took us to hear Sis. Jean Holland preach. Bro. Wiley Holland was with us. They always sang and Sis. Jean would play her guitar. I went with them to Monroe, Louisiana and stayed a week with them. I was so blessed to be with them.

Sis. Jean always wanted me to do her sewing. When she would come home from a revival she had 3 skirts for me to sew for her that were pleated. I was always proud to do them for her. Sis. Jean was always taking us places. Riding and telling us funny stories. She would take us to the A & W after church for root beer floats. One Christmas, when she and Arlene were working at a clothing shop in Natchez, MS, they took me and my 5 other sisters to the shop to buy us all a new coat for winter. I think the name of the shop was "Peggy's Dress Shop." I can remember my coat very well. It was pearl gray with push-up sleeves.

Faith Tabernacle had a live broadcast on "KFNV" AM Radio Station in Ferriday, Louisiana for a while on Sunday afternoons at 2:00 p.m. It was a 30 minute program. We would sing for about 15 minutes and then we would have someone preach for about 10 minutes. After a few months the radio station would bring their recording machines to the church and would record our program on Saturday afternoon. Then on Sunday afternoon they would play the program. All of us who participated really enjoyed that.

I remember Bro. Wiley Holland going with Daddy and Mama and us kids to fellowship meetings and different places. We would pass a cemetery. He would say in a soft voice, "You know people are dying to be in that place." Then he would laugh. We kids thought it was funny every time he said that.

Sometimes when Sis. Holland and Sis. Arlene would come home from revivals, they would come to our house. They would cook breakfast for Mama. Arlene would cook tomato gravy and biscuits, and Sis. Jean would bring Raspberry Kool-Aid. We all thought that was the best meal ever.

When I was young, I was sick a lot. I will always remember Bro. Holland coming to pray for me. It didn't matter if it was day or night, or any type of weather. He always came. I remember his gentle hand on my forehead. You couldn't help but feel better with those gentle hands praying for you.

One summer our family just got home from Oregon. We went to church with Mama and Daddy on a Sunday night. The young children would all sit along the platform for "children's church." The kids could say a Bible verse or sing. My oldest son, Kenneth Smart, got up to sing. My brother, J.E. Parker played the guitar for him to sing. I had no idea what he was planning to sing. He was only about 6 years old. He sang, "Silent Night." Now this is in the middle of June! Sis. Holland cried so hard from laughter. She had the whole church, including me, crying. I was as surprised as anyone.

Oh! My! And Easter! All of us teenagers would dress up to the nines! Of all the pretty dresses, hats, gloves, and heels. It was a beautiful sight to see. Kind of like a beautiful flower garden in full bloom. I can recall one Easter in particular. Charlotte and Leah, my sisters, had to take Easter baskets to the school for an Easter Egg Hunt. Mama and Daddy didn't have extra money to buy them baskets so Mama took 2 oatmeal boxes, covered them with crepe paper, and crafted a handle out of ribbons. She tore up tissue paper for grass, and placed the eggs carefully in the homemade baskets. Sis. Jean and Arlene came by to take them to school. They had a big surprise for my two little sisters. Sis. Jean had bought both of them a beautiful Easter Basket. You should have seen the pure joy on their little faces when they saw those baskets.

A library couldn't contain all the wonderful memories I have of the Hollands, the Vidalia church, and all that they meant to the Parker family. Sis. Jean Holland has been a great blessing and inspiration to all of us all through these years. I was asked by my sisters to write this chapter for Sis. Holland's third book "My Heritage." I can truly say that it has been my honor to do this. Sis. Holland is so much like her father, Bro. Wiley Holland. She has his sweet humble ways, and his gentle touch. She even has his sense of humor. Speaking on behalf of the entire Parker family, we could never fully tell or show how much we love you, Pastor Jean Holland. All our love for now and for always.

I'm Counting on You

By Casey Johnese

"I'm counting on you, Casey." Four words spoken by Pastor Dr. Jean Holland to me. These words pierced through my soul like a dagger. You might ask why, so I will explain. First of all, someone of her caliber counting on me? What she didn't know was at that exact moment; I was at a crossroads. I had received the baptism of the Holy Ghost a few months before and had experienced a beautiful and mighty deliverance from years of drug addiction and the hurtful and destructive life that comes with it. Even though I had felt the miraculous power of God; I was struggling to let go of the cigarette habit.

This particular night, I was in the car with my parents and we were heading home for the weekend. This would be in another town, so I thought I should call Pastor and let her know why I won't be in church. That was not the only thought I had in mind. As soon as I get off the phone, I'm smoking this cigarette. I haven't had one in a few weeks and I really need one. These were certainly my thoughts when I called Pastor and told her I was going out of town. When Pastor

Holland heard my plan she got real quiet. Then she said those words I will never forget, "I'm counting on you, Casey." She was telling me she believed in me! She had watched the cleansing power of Jesus work in my entire life. Her words spoke life into my soul. I knew that I would not; nor could not let this Pastor down. She believes in me. I did not smoke that cigarette that night and I haven't had one for 16 years now! When I gave that last addiction to the Lord in the backseat of that station wagon that night—He was ready to use me. Use me for His service and His Glory.

My sister, Kandy Coolman, started coming to visit our dad. She and her husband, Steve, were excited to introduce their first born son and my dad's grandson, Austin Coolman. God had a plan through this introduction. He wanted to bring healing and sweet redemption into our family. Kandy invited me to come to Richland and stay the weekend and fellowship with her and her family.

Let me share some facts about my life and background before being born again. When I was 18 years old, I began dancing and working in exotic clubs. Heavy drug use and drinking alcohol excessively was an everyday thing for me and those I was running with. It was the norm. I was introduced to drugs/alcohol and all the rituals that come along with that lifestyle through my family—upon birth.

My dad was a country music song writer and entertainer so I started the night club scene by the age of around 10 years old. Soon after, I started to fight at school because kids made fun of me and my dirt-poor family. By 7th grade, I was a well-respected fighter and known for standing up for not only myself but anyone who was bullied and made fun of. I would always take my shoes off as a mental preparation for the fight that I was engaging in. The "shoes off" reputation followed me even now into almost being 40 years old. It was the JNT youth's theme for the 2016 New Year: shoes off, it's time to fight! Now I know who the real enemy is.

After several visits to see Kandy, my twin sisters, Kathryn and Rhonda, and visiting JNT church, God began breaking the shell of hurt and anger that covered my hard sinful heart. I called my mom one morning after I had worked all night in a strip club in Jackson. "Casey," she said, "your twin sisters are having a birthday party at "that church" on Hwy 49 they all go to." I need to mention that my mother was not their mother as my father had divorced and remarried so they were my half-sisters. "Go by there," she suggested.

I remember stopping at a bathroom and washing my face from a night of hard drugs, demonic music, and drinking. I went by TJ Max and bought the twins some birthday gifts. I remember walking in the youth center that day to one of the warmest greetings I've ever received in my life. It was as if Jesus Himself hugged me and said, "Welcome home, Casey. We've been waiting for you!" I'll never forget one of the smiles that day that caught my attention—Sis. Patti Gordon smiled at me and it was as if Jesus Himself smiled at me.

Through the course of a couple of years, my life began to spiral quickly out of control. I would call out to Kandy in drunken stupors—I knew I had a refuge—a place of hope. I got in trouble with the law and couldn't stay sober enough to work and pay the probation officer or the fines any longer. The probation officer was ready to lock me up—her name happened to be Kandy, too. I was living from pillar to post in Petal. Because of extreme anger outburst no one wanted to be around me anymore. I was also broke, had no pocket full of dope, nice apartment or fast car anymore. Without those things, I didn't feel worthy to surround myself with people because those things made me feel powerful. The Lord stripped those things away from me. Godly sorrow began to work real repentance

> *2 Corinthians 7:10 For godly sorrow worketh repentance to salvation not to be repented of: but the sorrow of the world worketh death.*

I called out to Kandy over and over, and she always came to my rescue. I told my dad I was going to stay with her for a while, get a job, and pay my fines off. As I began to stay with them in their home, I began the process of being delivered from the stronghold that the devil had on me.

> *2 Corinthians 10:4 (For the weapons of our warfare are not carnal, but mighty through God to the pulling down of strong holds;)*

> *Ephesians 6:12 For we wrestle not against flesh and blood, but against principalities, against powers, against the rulers of the darkness of this world, against spiritual wickedness in high places.*

I would be awakened at night by an evil presence and would feel like someone was choking me. I was determined to attend church every time Kandy and the family went. Satan and my calloused heart had convinced me I was "saved." Then, one red hot Mississippi Sunday night July 25, 1999, God's love and mercy miraculously reached into my heart. My brother-in-law, Reverend Steve Coolman preached a message straight from God's heart that night, "The Value of the Broken." He talked about the broken alabaster box—the beautiful fragrance was not released until the box was broken.

> *Mark 14:3 And being in Bethany in the house of Simon the leper, as he sat at meat, there came a woman having an alabaster box of ointment of spikenard very precious; and she brake the box, and poured it on his head*

He mentioned how the Apostle Paul and others held on to the broken pieces of the ship and made it safely to the shore.

Acts 27:44 And the rest, some on boards, and some on broken pieces of the ship. And so it came to pass, that they escaped all safe to land

God let me know that night there was value in my broken, sinful life. Conviction pierced deeply into my heart. I reached down and removed my shoes. I knew it was time to fight the addictions and I needed God as my corner man! That night I did the 3 step program! I stepped out of pew, stepped into that altar (repentance), and then stepped into the baptistery! I went down in that water in Jesus Name! Pastor Holland was standing at that baptistery and informed me that when I went down in that water every sin I had ever committed would be washed away—that I would be a brand new creature in Christ! Bro. Steve baptized me and when I came out of the water I was speaking in an unknown tongue!

Acts 2:38 Then Peter said unto them, Repent, and be baptized every one of you in the name of Jesus Christ for the remission of sins, and ye shall receive the gift of the Holy Ghost.

A mighty, mighty deliverance took place instantly! A new creature indeed was born—and I began to witness to people everywhere I went! No one was spared from hearing my testimony when I walked into a room! A few months later, after Pastor Holland said, "I'm counting on you"—I had surely quit smoking, but there were destructive ties with people and family in my home town. Not anymore!! Not only was Pastor Holland counting on me but I knew that my Savior and King was also counting on me. Little did I realize the lost souls that God would reach out to and set free because of my testimony.

I was invited to come back to Petal High School to share my testimony with all of the staff there. The ones who thought I was a hopeless case got to hear how God delivered my life from that horrible pit (Psalm 43). They gave me a standing ovation that day. But, it was Jesus that I gave that standing ovation to.

Psalms 40:2 He brought me up also out of an horrible pit, out of the miry clay, and set my feet upon a rock, and established my goings.

Sis. Nancy Howell's ministered in the JNT youth group. She taught us with such conviction that every Sunday morning was a revival service. We had Tuesday night Bible study and Saturday night prayer meetings that would sometimes last all night! We fasted weekly and did outreach regularly. God cleaned up my mouth and emotional hangups disappeared the more I fasted and prayed.

Within a year, I met a Christian man, Jimmy Johnese, and we started to date. We dated for nearly a year and then we were married. Eight years later God gave us a miracle in having our only daughter, Lola Faith Johnese, who is now 7 years old. I am so thankful for a godly husband, who preaches and teaches God's Word, and a beautiful daughter.

Jimmy and his brother, Justin, attended Faith Tabernacle in Louisiana where Bro. George Guy pastored during the earlier years of their life. Brother Guy is Pastor Holland's nephew. When the family moved to Florence, MS to live with their uncle they made the connection at school with my sister Kathryn. Their mother, Kathy, had lived with Pastor Holland part of her life. Jimmy and Justin's grandparents, Jean and Jimmy Skeen, were earlier members of JNT. God really placed the pieces together perfectly! Justin married Theresa Tune, a young lady that had been at JNT with her family since she was about 12 years old. They have a handsome son, Beckett, and a beautiful daughter, Chloe-Jayne.

After a few years, I enrolled in college and completed a program to become a certified Drug/Alcohol counselor. Within 2 months of enrolling, God opened the door wide for me to become a counselor at a local treatment center for women. The ladies there loved coming to church at JNT and we prayed hundreds of them through and baptized many. One Sunday night, 12 of them received the Holy Ghost!

God opened the door for me to go back home to Petal and preach several revivals. One lasted 6 weeks! We had around 25 receive the Holy Ghost in that revival with 9 receiving the Holy Ghost in the first weekend of the revival! Friends, I did drugs with, came to hear me preach high on drugs, but left talking in tongues!

Pastor Holland evangelized many years before becoming the Pastor of Jesus Name Tabernacle. She has a deep desire to see souls saved and set free from the devils bondage. She teaches us how to evangelize successfully. The minister's suppers she conducts are designed for her to give us her insights and training for successful revivals. She is a revivalist who loves lost souls and teaches us to do the same! Her love for souls no doubt played the major part in my dad receiving the Holy Ghost at Jesus Name Tabernacle when he was 73 years old.

Sis. Nancy told the story one Sunday morning of a great crisis that happened on a beach. Because of the tides, thousands of star fish were washed up and were dying on the beach. An onlooker saw a man walking along picking up one starfish at a time and tossing it back into the sea. The onlooker yelled, "Sir! There's too many to save! What you're doing won't make a difference!" The man picked up a starfish and tossed it into the sea and said, "I made a difference for that one!" I am that star fish JNT picked up and tossed back to sea!

> *2 Peter 1:11 For so an entrance shall be ministered unto you abundantly into the everlasting kingdom of our Lord and Saviour Jesus Christ.*

Throughout the course of my conversion, I lived with Steve and Kandy Coolman, Norma Langston, and Max and Peggy Smith. The instruction, nurturing, and love I've received from this congregation is truly what soul winning is all about! This is the kind of soul winning that Pastor Holland longs for and teaches us to long for. Jesus said we are made overcomers by our testimony.

> *Revelation 12:11 And they overcame him by the blood of the Lamb, and by the word of their testimony; and they loved not their lives unto the death.*

I love the words of the beautiful hymn by John Newton:

Amazing grace (how sweet the sound) that saved a wretch like me! I once was lost, but now am found, was blind, but now I see. 'Twas grace that taught my heart to fear, and grace my fears relieved; how precious did that grace appear the hour I first believed! Through many dangers, toils and snares I have already come: 'tis grace has brought me safe thus far, and grace will lead me home. The Lord has promised good to me, his word my hope secures; he will my shield and portion be as long as life endures. Yes, when this flesh and heart shall fail, and mortal life shall cease: I shall possess, within the veil, a life of joy and peace. The earth shall soon dissolve like snow, the sun forbear to shine; but God, who called me here below, will be forever mine.

My (Space) Story

By Josh Palmer

In this day of social networking, it may be hard to believe that this is not a brand new concept. Though the delivery and method have changed, and certainly the time span…it is not foreign to this world. And in the spirit of that, I present to you My(Space) Story.

First of all, I will prove my point of social networking not being a new concept the following way…

Matthew 28: 19—20 [19] "Go ye therefore, and teach all nations, baptizing them in the name of the Father, and of the Son, and of the Holy Ghost:" [20] "Teaching them to observe all things whatsoever I have commanded you: and, lo, I am with you alway, even unto the end of the world. Amen."

Luke 14:23 [23] "And the lord said unto the servant, Go out into the highways and hedges, and compel them to come in, that my house may be filled."

This does not begin in "space," but rather MySpace. Some may be too young or too far removed to remember this, but it was a precedent of FaceBook. While wildly popular, momentum was lost with the inception of the latter. And I suppose people continue to use it today, it has lost a good bit of traction. But back then, it was the go—to social network. And it was here, I would be connected to the greatest moments of my life so far, with more to come.

It was a normal day for me as I was at work. Quick backstory. I had been out of high school and college since 2003. So it had been almost 4 yours since I had any real friends around. Not to say that I wasn't loved, but I had to face it…marriage, children, careers, etc…had taken their toll on my friendships. I suppose I was a bit lonely, and life had become dull and routine. I often wondered where and how I might meet a girl or even more friends. Especially being that I never did anything. My days were spent at work then home to my parent's house where I had recently moved back in. I had a great relationship with them, but let's face it, who wants to hang out with Mom and Dad constantly and what Mom and Dad doesn't want their son to find love and friends? My nights were spent at home and my weekends the same. I wasn't depressed or anything of the sort. Just simply alone. My greatest joy was when I knew I would have the house to myself for the weekend because parents were out of town. But really this only meant watching baseball if in season or football and if neither was available, watching a movie. But I enjoyed the time alone. And as it would be, that time alone always left me longing for more. I knew something was missing in my life, but other than a real career and a wife, I didn't know what. I just kept on day to day wondering; growing ever more anxious. Little did I know, as we all are sometimes, that I was being prepared to meet the greatest friend(s) I've ever known, while also gaining a second family.

Now, back to that normal day. I was at work and on a break, or maybe not, I don't know... I was wandering around this MySpace. I had a simple little page with mostly old friends from high school. But really, most of these people I had not seen for 6 or 7 years. But they were there nonetheless. And we all know that all your friends on social networking are friends for life, right...? So, this day there was an invitation posted publicly for anyone not busy that Wednesday night, to come to church service at JNT. Now, I cannot tell you how many times I had driven by that church. Really probably every day for years. And during high school, I wasn't really friends with Kathryn (as I knew her) or Rhonda Prine. I knew them and we had homeroom together, but that was it. So, for about 15 minutes each school day, I had a class with them. But that was really the extent of the relationship. However, this invitation led to me thinking... "Hmmm. I can go to this church and reconnect with some old "friends" and I'll feel better." So I took the bait and asked some questions. Finding out that a few other people I knew from high school were attending there as well.

It was still a few weeks before I got around to going. And when I did, I pulled up one night and there was no service, but a children's program rehearsal. I was greeted by Bro. Dana who invited me in and was warm and kind, but I declined, stating I would come back when there was a service. It was still a few weeks before I went back, but another normal day happened. As I was driving home from work, I noticed all the power was out in Florence and there was no reason for it. No bad weather, no pole was struck, nothing. But it was definitely out. And I hated when the power was out because as a (we'll say fluffy) person, I tend to get hot easily. So I decided I was not going to sit at home and burn up. Ironic how that decision may have well served to keep me from burning up for eternity. So, I got home, got dressed, and drove up to JNT. There I was greeted by the same Bro. Dana, and I was so impressed he even remembered my name from a few weeks before. Then I was further greeted by hugs from Kathryn and Rhonda and a bountiful of handshakes throughout the night. This further impressed me. I had searched for church after church off and on throughout my life, but none even compared to the friendliness and love felt here. I was introduced around, even welcomed from the platform when the twins got up to sing. These things may not be a big deal or seem like much to you, but to me, they meant the world. I was even a little scared of the amount of love shown. I was definitely not used to it.

I continued to come, but only on Wednesday night. My weekends were reserved for deer camp and hunting. For a few months this continued. I was invited to Sunday School eventually by Bro. Max (who would go on to become a mentor). And I was more welcomed there. I had no preconceived notions about Pentecost before arriving, but it was a very new experience. And because of my longingness to belong and be accepted, I guess I was a perfect candidate to receive the Holy Ghost. I was chasing after something I didn't even know I was chasing.

After adding Sunday to my church regimen, I had no idea that God was building my ministry. I had no desire to preach or teach or sing or anything. I honestly just thought this church would be a passing phase. I thought I would get my feel of it and move on. But God began to plant roots for me that I could not even see. He used numerous people to help me along the way, but I have to give a special acknowledgement to one couple. And I know I will get chastised for it, but I have a point to it and it is worth it. Matt and Kat Cooper were the two most influential people in my life beginning here. The times we spent together just talking about God and this life. The things I had to learn and realize. The guidance by two people who had lived this way their whole life was just invaluable.

It was immeasurable. I would venture to say that if not for them, I may not have even stayed as long as I did. But for fear of embarrassing them, I'll move on to return briefly at another point. God was building this ministry for me and me alone. He has a unique one for us all. As I grew, I was told that God was going to use me and so on…I just sort of brushed it off as people being nice. And as I moved forward, I was given opportunities to teach as part of a tag team in Sunday School. I do not claim to be now, and was not then, a good teacher. And I cannot say I feel called to teach. That is a special gift. But it was very necessary for me to learn and progress. After all, I had only been in this truth for 3 years, so there were and still is today, a tremendous amount for me to learn. I had a message or a thought, however you want to label it, that I just could not get out of my head. Another friend of mine, whom emailed back and forth throughout most days, encouraged me to tell Pastor Holland I had a message. I battled saying, no she will come to me when she feels I am ready. But I was continually encouraged by this friend. So, to my reluctance I called my pastor and told her I felt like I had a message. To this day, I will never forget her response. She simply replied, "I thought you might…" And at that point, I realized that she knew and was waiting for me.

Not long after that, I began that phase of my ministry behind the pulpit. I say this all to say, I am not claiming to now be a great preacher, or even a good one. I am certainly not claiming to be anything bigger. But I can say, with a tremendous smile, that I am doing a work for God. I chose to make myself available and God used me. This is not to mean that haven't failed and do not fail daily. But I should be no better than Paul said and not die daily. But over this very short time, I have seen and learned of God's grace and mercy. I have seen the importance of reaching out. I have seen the fruits of so many labors. And I have seen that the smallest of invitations, that you most likely think will reach nobody, can be the one that saves even one soul. I am a first generation Apostolic Pentecost. But every generation has to start somewhere. And however long my legacy may or may not last, I know that I have something great, something both tangible and intangible, something easy to grasp but surpasses all understanding to hand down to my children. And just as I opened my very first message as a single man with these words "I would like to say I love my wife, whoever she is…" I will say here that I love my kids whenever they come, and cannot wait to hand this down to them.

And God, obviously did reveal my wife to me a short time later. And just as proudly as I could say it that day, I am able to say it much more that I love her. She has been a constant and consistent partner and help meet. She has been my biggest fan and encourager through all we've gone through. And at the time God was preparing my ministry, He was also preparing hers. I am very proud of who she is and what she stands for. You never have to question. And I have no idea what the future holds for us but I do know Who holds us in the future. And I am so eternally grateful for the lady he sent me and allowed me to walk through this life with. He is, indeed, a thoughtful God.

In closing, I encourage each and every one of you to just send out that invitation. As small as you may think or as little as you may believe you will reach. You never know when you may bring in Abraham and all his seed or even just a single Paul to help spread the word. And I am in no way comparing myself or my family to these great men, but even if one soul,

one person, one heart gets turned to One God, One Accord, One Place then it was all worth it. God gives us the tools to use to reach out. And whether it be MySpace, Facebook, or some other social network. Or just good old fashioned door knocking…you could very well be the person to bring in a new generation, who will one day proclaim… "I didn't know where I was going. I didn't know what I was doing. But now I have a purpose. Now I see a place for me. And now I have my space reserved in His book."

The Lady....Jean Holland

By VaLynn Mills

VaLynn Scheel and her parents had an opportunity to officially meet Sis. Jean Holland in 1987. Sis. Holland had a magnetic personality and VaLynn immediately bonded with her.

The following year, VaLynn was one of the senior graduates at Lighthouse Christian Academy in Beebe, Arkansas. She was thrilled when the class all agreed that Sis. Jean Holland would be the guest speaker for this very special occasion. Sis. Holland brought a touch of "class" like no other! Not only was she an eloquent speaker, but she could relate to anyone at any level. She presented each graduate with a beautiful leather Bible that was autographed and it had an awesome quote that will be forever engraved not only in the Bible, but in the hearts of the graduates. "This book will keep you from sin; and sin will keep you from this book."

VaLynn enjoyed her frequent trips to Florence and cherished every moment with Sis. Holland. They made great memories as they would attend the annual JCM Music Conference, UPC Mississippi Camp

Meeting and other events. They also enjoyed quality time by the lake on Sis. Holland's property. During each visit, VaLynn would learn something new from Sis. Holland. She always had a fun story to share and with each story, was a lesson to be learned.

Sis. Holland once shared that she was always taught to never accept a false prophecy from anyone. Their church was in a revival and someone wanted to pray over her and told her God was going to heal her headaches. She had NEVER had a headache in her life! She told the preacher that she had never had a headache and wasn't going to accept one now! She told VaLynn and the girls that they better be the same way and never accept something that was not true.

Sis. Holland is a world class chef and would call VaLynn and share her new recipes. She also introduced some fine dining spots in Jackson. It was truly amazing that people in every restaurant knew Sis. Holland and they would roll out the red carpet for her and her guests. From Cock of the Walk, to Char's and even the fast food chains! Again, that awesome magnetic personality and the queen of tipping made an impression on the waiters.

In 1994, VaLynn and Dustin Mills announced their engagement and both agreed that Sis. Jean Holland would be the one to perform the wedding ceremony. She provided good, godly council and presented them with their first family Bible. Once again, she performed a ceremony like none other!

Sis. Jean Holland has played an important role with the Scheel and Mills families through every season of life. Any time there was a problem, big or small, Sis. Holland was always there to listen and encourage, providing great advice.

The Lighthouse in Beebe suffered a great loss during the horrific tornado that destroyed the church and campus. The tornado also picked up VaLynn while driving her car. Sis. Jean Holland was the first person VaLynn called. It was through conversations with Sis. Holland one could find the strength and courage to keep pressing on. Soon following the tornado, Sis. Holland came to visit and preached in the temporary church location, which was a car dealership.

The Lighthouse annual church conference was a time when we knew we could count on Sis. Holland and some of her church family to attend and participate. Sis. Holland preached at several conferences and always had an incredible testimony and song to share. Her anointed singing would move a crowd and the power of God would bless the entire congregation. Sis. Holland accompanied the Lighthouse Choir one year by singing one of her most famous songs "Get Away Jordan."

When Dustin and VaLynn decided to start a family, one of the first calls made was to share the news with Sis. Holland. She was so excited and would follow up on VaLynn to be sure she was doing good. At 32 weeks, VaLynn had some major complications and had to have an emergency C-section. Hackler weighed 3 lb., 13 oz. and had to be transported by med-flight to Arkansas Children's Hospital in Little Rock. Hackler was on life support, had a hole in his heart and his lungs were not fully developed. This was a very difficult trial, and they didn't know if Hackler would live or die. VaLynn was in the White County Hospital in Searcy, which was an hour from Little Rock. Sis. Holland and Sis. Nancy surprised VaLynn the very next day, and walked into the hospital to check on her! They both went to see Hackler after their visit with VaLynn.

Hackler received a miracle and was released from the hospital four weeks following his arrival! Sis. Holland made another trip to Beebe to participate in Hackler's special Baby Dedication Service. She bought Hackler his first Bible and performed a beautiful ceremony.

In 2004, VaLynn and Dustin announced they were expecting another baby in November. Once again, the call was made to Sis. Holland. She was so excited! When they went for an ultra sound, they found out that they were expecting twin boys! VaLynn called Sis. Holland from the clinic to share the shocking news!

On July 6, VaLynn went into labor and she was at 25 weeks with the twins. Unfortunately, the twins didn't make it. The family was devastated and Sis. Holland immediately made a trip to Beebe. The family found great strength in her comforting words as she spoke at the twins' funeral.

VaLynn reconnected with a friend in Louisiana in December 2004. She told her about the opportunity to adopt a baby that was due in March 2005. VaLynn contacted Sis. Holland, so that she could pray for the situation. Sis. Holland and VaLynn remained in close contact as the adoption process continued.

On March 8th (the day before Sis. Holland's birthday), Hannidy Carter Mills was born! What an incredible experience for VaLynn and Dustin as they got to be at the hospital in Shreveport for his delivery.

Sis. Holland drove to Beebe and assisted with Hannidy's Baby Dedication Service. What a beautiful ceremony for our first adopted Lighthouse baby!

The Lighthouse Church in Beebe celebrated their 50th church anniversary in April 2016. Sis. Holland

had suffered a stroke and was recovering. Although the doctor suggested that Sis. Holland not travel, she was determined to surprise VaLynn and her church family by showing up for the final night of this special celebration.

As you can see, Sis. Holland has been a true friend in the good times and also in the bad times. Although VaLynn says that they were not born into the same family, they are really sisters of the heart and will always be like family. The closeness that is shared is amazing. She is consistent and the best friend anyone could ever want.

Light of God

By Elizabeth Loper

Matthew 5:16 Let your light so shine before men, that they may see your good works, and glorify your Father which is in heaven.

One day my husband, Wayne, and I went to the income tax office. We were waiting our turn to go into the office and I noticed a lady with her little boy. They were sitting across from me and near where Wayne was seated. After a while they moved over on the couch next to me. The Lady was talking to her son about some pictures on the table. I could feel something as I watched them. "What church do you attend?" I asked. "Jesus Named Tabernacle on Highway 49," she answered.

We began to talk and I shared with her how much I wanted to find a church to attend. Wayne had experienced a stroke, and I mentioned that I knew God allowed him to live and definitely had a reason for his recovery.

This godly lady was Peggy Smith. She reached into her purse and handed me a church card. The times for the services, phone number, address and Pastor Jean Holland's picture was on the card. Services were on Wednesday night, Sunday morning, and Sunday night.

As Wayne and I started home, I told him that we needed to start going to church. We needed to go somewhere and I believed this church was the one I want to go to. We drove down Highway 49 and saw where the church was located. A couple of weeks passed by and we still hadn't made it to any of the services. One Saturday I told Wayne, "I'm going to church in the morning." He said, "Okay."

I was already familiar with Pentecostal churches and how they worship. In Louisiana, my daddy and mother used to go to different churches and preach. During that time, I had married and lived in Texas. I was raised Baptist and I knew the difference in Baptist and Pentecostal churches was as different as day—light and dark, or at least the ones I had attended were.

All my life I had heard it preached that church was a place to go if you said you were saved, or if you wanted to be saved. Sin was something that everyone does and God understood we were sinners saved by grace. That's true but I knew that God wanted more than lip service. A born again child of God will think and act differently. I knew that and I saw in Mrs. Peggy Smith the quality I hungered for.

The truth is that before a person obeys Acts 2:38, we don't have power to live a holy life.

Acts 2:38-40 Then Peter said unto them, Repent, and be baptized every one of your in the name of Jesus Christ for the remission of sins, and ye shall receive the gift of the Holy Ghost. For the promise is unto you, and to your children, and to all that are afar off, even as many as the Lord our God shall call. And with many other words did he testify, and exhort, saying, Save yourselves from this untoward generation.

Before a person receives the baptism of the Holy Ghost and is baptized in Jesus Name they might think they're living right. I'm not putting down other churches, but the Bible is the only way, and that is what I found at Jesus Name Tabernacle. I thought I was living the right way until I received what Jesus did for me; so I'm going to tell everyone I meet what happened to me.

I had been attending services and enjoying them so very much. One Sunday evening Wayne didn't go to church with me. He just wasn't feeling well, but it was fine with him for me to go on to service. I was sitting there on the pew by myself and Sister Peggy's mom, Sis Nancy Howell, came over and sat with me. I knew why she was there. They had made the altar call. The second time they asked if anyone wanted to come to the altar I asked if she would go with me. She jumped up like she had springs in her shoes. Sister Peggy's husband Brother Max joined us at the altar. I was gloriously filled with the Holy

Ghost. When I got home, Wayne looked at me and said, "You got the Holy Ghost, didn't you?" He could feel it.

Brother Max said he would like to baptize both of us together in the precious name of Jesus at the same time. I was surely ready but I also wanted to wait on Wayne. I felt in my heart that there was more. I desired to obey the word of God. One Sunday night, Brother Johnny Roney preached and the Lord touched Wayne's heart and he went to the altar. He received the baptism of the Holy Ghost, and we were both baptized in the wonderful name of Jesus. When I went under the water it felt like all my sins went with me, and when I came out and the water parted I was free with a new life.

I will always be thankful for people God used to set me free of all my sinful ways. I continually thank God for these people who showed me the Bible way to be saved. It placed a hunger and thirst in my soul to study God's word and be faithful to God's house and witness to everyone I know.

> Sister Peggy Smith — the godly witness who invited me to JNT.
> Sister Nancy Howell (Sister Peggy's mother) — has been the anointed example to her children and grandchildren.
> Brother Max Smith (Sister Peggy's husband) — who would become the pastor of JNT.

Thank you Pastor Jean Holland — no one could be a godlier, powerful minister of the Gospel. Thank you Jesus my Savior and Redeemer — You came to this lost sheep and led me to the truth.

When I think and meditate about the night I received the Holy Ghost, it was the most wonderful experience that had ever happened to me. I was being held with the loving arms of Jesus around me and he said, "Well done, my child." Later I was baptized in Jesus Name and that also was such a wonderful feeling. I knew I had been washed clean of all my sins. I was a new babe in Christ. Like Jesus told Nicodemas, I was born again of the water and the spirit.

John 3:5 Jesus answered, Verily verily, I say unto thee, Except a man be born of water and of the Spirit, he cannot enter into the kingdom of God.

The Lord gave us his word to read and study. We pray and obey the Lord. Worshiping is our way to grow and be like Jesus. I'm still a new babe in Christ, and I have a lot to learn.

One thing for sure if it had not been for the lady speaking to me in a gentle voice that day in the tax office and inviting me to church I might still be a lost soul. I knew when she sat down I wanted to talk, and I wanted to go where she went to church. She was a blessing to me and I so appreciate her taking time to give a card with phone numbers and times for the services at Jesus Name Tabernacle. My sister had prayed that God would send someone to my door. He did, but it was different. It was my heart's door.

You know some people don't believe that there is a heaven or a hell. They think that when you die you're buried and that's all there is to it. That is just the beginning. If you're not ready to meet Jesus, it will be bad. I'm so glad that I finally saw the light. When you repent and receive the Holy Ghost and get baptized, that is just the beginning. I found out when I read my Bible and pray, I get closer to Jesus each and every day. When I worship the Lord I am so blessed. When it is my time to go, I hope, I trust and pray, that I will be holding my daddy's hand and I will hear Jesus say, "Go through the pearly gates, my child."

Honor Christ in Your Service

By Lisa Blaine

Mark 14:3-9 And being in Bethany in the house of Simon the leper, as he sat at meat, there came a woman having an alabaster box of ointment of spikenard very precious; and she brake the box, and poured it on his head.

And there were some that had indignation within themselves, and said, why was this waste of the ointment made? *For it might have been sold for more than three hundred pence, and have been given to the poor. And they murmured against her. And Jesus said, "Let her alone; why trouble ye her? She hath wrought a good work on me. For ye have the poor with you always, and whensoever ye will ye may do them good: but me ye have not always. She hath done what she could: she is come aforehand to anoint my body to the burying. Verily I say unto you, Wheresoever this gospel shall be preached throughout the whole world, this also that she hath done shall be spoken of for a memorial of her."*

The same action was considered a waste by some, but not by Jesus. No doubt she did not fully comprehend the depth of worship in her action. "She hath wrought a good work on me," Jesus said. Waste or worship? This depends on the heart of the individual. In this passage of scripture, the woman's worship was sacrificial, humble, and pure. Others who witnessed the pouring out of the precious ointment could think of nothing other than it was a waste. Why did they murmur and complain? Where did their indignation come from?

Did their attitude prevent her? She knew whose feet she was anointing. She was only concerned with honoring Jesus and not what others thought. Her beautiful sacrifice has been used by the Holy Ghost to bless all who love the Lord. Often our worship and service is hindered by our fear of what others think. Possibly this is one of the reasons our acts toward the Lord are not remembered. She was remembered wherever the Gospel is preached because she was doing it for an audience of one! This motive made the difference in her service and it will make the difference in ours.

Luke 22:26-27 But ye shall not be so: but he that is greatest among you, let him be as the younger; and he that is chief, as he that doth serve. For whether is greater, he that sitteth at meat, or he that serveth? is not he that sitteth at meat? but I am among you as he that serveth.

In Jesus day the washing of feet was a task reserved

not just for the servants but the very lowest of servants. In these verses the one with the towel and basin is the King of the Universe. He not only calls Himself the one that serves but He is our example. Hours before Jesus would be crucified He taught the New Commandment.

John 13:34 A new commandment I give unto you, That ye love one another; as I have loved you, that ye also love one another.

Jesus concern is twofold. More than removing dirt, Jesus is removing doubt. Jesus was revealing to them that if they knew Him the way they said then they would serve one another. His desire was for the disciples to know how much he loves them. As Christians we are deeply loved by God, and His love spills over to others. God's love is the force and flow behind Christian service.

1 John 4:16 And we have known and believed the love that God hath to us. God is love; and he that dwelleth in love dwelleth in God, and God in him.

Without a Savior, without a changed heart, and without the Holy Ghost to comfort, teach, and guide us we would still be under His wrath. This love propels us to serve. Without His love and our adoration for Him our serving becomes a joyless duty. Our appreciation for what Jesus did for us when He took our sins and became the perfect sacrifice motivates us to love Him and to love others. By serving others we are also blessed.

Luke 6:38 Give, and it shall be given unto you; good measure, pressed down, shaken together, and running over, shall men give into your bosom. For with the same measure that ye mete withal it shall be measured to you again.

God's love moves on us to serve the widow and the fatherless. In our service we are able to serve people the way we would want to be treated. We are able to love those who may not love us.

Psalm 100:2 Serve the LORD with gladness: come before his presence with singing.

Colossians 3:23-24 And whatsoever ye do, do it heartily, as to the Lord, and not unto men; Knowing that of the Lord ye shall receive the reward of the inheritance: for ye serve the Lord Christ.

Galatians 5:13 For, brethren, ye have been called unto liberty; only use not liberty for an occasion to the flesh, but by love serve one another.

Senior Pastor, Dr. Jean Holland, taught me these truths first hand. She is a perfect example of a true servant of God. No other person has influenced me to have a servant's heart as much as she has. Nothing has as much impact as a Godly example and everything I have said thus far is a result of her teaching. She is that and so much more. Not just once or twice but always.

It is a great privilege to write a chapter in her book about treasuring treasures. She is a treasure to me. She holds fast to the truths of God's Word. Acts 2:38, and living a Holy Godly life is her pattern. Dr. Holland manifests the fruit of the Spirit. Love, Joy, Peace, Longsuffering, Gentleness, faith, Meekness and Temperance flow in her life. Her Christ-like example of leadership is balanced with her servant's heart. She loves all people. Great, small, rich, poor, saints and sinners. Like the woman with the alabaster box, her Savior is the one who she wants to receive glory and honor. She gives of herself sacrificially and makes herself available to the hurting and the lost. She visits the shut—ins bringing them food. Seeking to brighten their day. Her motto is, "win them with love."

I am deeply grateful to have benefited from her preaching, teaching, friendship, counsel, and servant's heart. She is without a doubt "real" and teaches others what that really means. Integrity is a must. One of her quotes is to take a little honey with us wherever we go, meaning to be kind to all. During the thirty years Dr. Holland pastored JNT with the many ministries involved, she preached conferences, cooked, fundraised, cut the lawn, fasted and prayed, helped with missions, and more.

The song writer said, "Thank you for giving to the Lord, I am a life that has been changed."

Thank you Sister Irma Jean Holland. I love you my shepherd, my friend.

My Greatest Influences

By Camille Gordon

*"And Ruth said, Intreat me not to leave thee,
or to return from following after thee..."*

It all began on February 27th, 2001. I was born to Donald and Patti Gordon. My mom told me that when I was born, I was screaming and crying, but when the doctor laid me on her chest, I immediately fell into a peaceful sleep. I was a whopping nine pounds and six ounces. I had thick, jet black hair. I still have the picture to this day of the first moment my parents held me in their arms. As a newborn, I could never have imagined how much I would love, cherish and respect them. I was certainly blessed to be born in the Gordon family.

Four months later, I was dedicated by Dr. Jean Holland. She has been very important in my life and in the lives of my entire family. Sis. Jean has been my pastor for all of my life, and such a firm foundation for my family and me. I can remember fearful times of sitting in a lonely hospital with different family members, and when she would walk in, I would feel the peace of God reassure me that everything was going to be alright. I'm thankful for the Godly walk she has and the impact she has on my life.

A short time passed and on July 30th, 2002, my sister, Claire, was born. I loved her the very second I laid eyes on her, and we became the very best of friends. A few years later, my personality started to evolve and I began to learn new things. At an early age, I would grab a small Bible that we had and stand on the hearth of our fireplace and pretend to preach. I have always had a passion for preaching, I loved watching people preach and I always dreamed of doing it one day. When I was about six years old, I was in art class at school. My art teacher, Mrs. Wolf, asked the class to draw a picture of what they wanted to be when they grew up. As I looked around the room, most students were drawing doctors, firemen, policemen, and teachers. I began to draw what first came to my mind, me standing on a platform behind a podium speaking to a congregation.

As the teacher made her way to each student, a smile appeared on her face. She slowly made her way to my table, a different look came across her face. "What are you doing in this picture?" she asked nicely. I replied, "I am speaking to my church." Her eyes lit up with excitement. She said, "How beautiful." She picked up my drawing and wrote "When I grow up, I will be... a minister." I still have that picture, my mom displays it on our refrigerator.

A few months later, I was in a Sunday night service and the choir was singing. My dad was leading to one of my favorite songs...

"Every time I think about you, Every time I read about you, Every time I hear your name, I start to smile. Every time the sun starts shining, Every time the wind starts blowing, Every time I feel your anointing, I start to smile. I'm in love with Jesus and he's in love with me."
(Timothy Wright, New Direction)

Without worrying about anyone else in the room, I closed my eyes and lifted my little hands up and began to feel a presence like none other before. I opened my mouth and started to speak with other tongues. I could feel the love of my mom, dad and many others around me as they were praying. From that night forward, I was changed. I never looked at church the same way. Everything took on a new meaning. When I came to church, the songs and preaching felt and sounded so different. It seemed like I was more in tune. That same year, I was baptized in Jesus Name. As a mere six year old, my sins were not many, I felt so spotless and white as snow.

From the innocent eyes of a six year old who only sees the good in the world, through the years there was an unveiling of what the world could really be like. As I began to mature, the world began to seem much more wicked and sinful to me. It wasn't always a pretty place. I began to feel what the attacks of peer pressure were like. I would go to school with so many negative influences around me daily, as I was picked up by my mom at the end of each day, I felt weighed down and dirty. I felt so heavy that I remember it being hard at times to even lift my hands in church. It had been so long since I had prayed or read my Bible. I wasn't living a sinful life, it just seemed that the negativity clouded my vision. There seemed to be such a distance from the little innocent six year old girl that Sunday night in church. Through that distance I felt, I learned what it was to fear, doubt and feel lonely in a sense. In what I thought felt like just going through the motions, I could hear God calling me to draw close to him.

As God's call grew stronger, a new hunger began to be restored in my heart. Despite all of the ungodly influences around me, I began to appreciate all of the Godly influences he placed in my life, such as...my parents, family, church family, and friends. It wasn't too much longer that in June 2014, Sis. Tammy Moak encouraged us to go to senior camp for the first time. It was such a life changing week for me. It was so amazing to be around many other young people seeking God. There was a real breakthrough in my walk with God after that week, but there was something much stronger tugging at my heart. My desire increased to read my bible, pray and fast more. I wanted to know God more. As I read his word more, the more I wanted to share it with others. This is when I was reminded of the dream I had as a child, and that was to become a minister.

I felt like my walk with the Lord was growing

stronger. Bro. Max and Sister Peggy were our youth pastors, and they would teach us to step out and be a worshipper. We are the Firestarters, so therefore, we should lead in the worship. Come out from our pew and be an example. My nana, Sis. Diane Gordon, would always encourage me to be an example and not be afraid to worship. After a while I started to do this each service and then it became hard to stay in my pew and not step out. I am thankful for their encouragement to become a true worshipper. It has made a huge difference in my life.

My desire to be used by the Lord through speaking became stronger than it had ever been. However, like anyone who wants to be used, there comes some doubt. I began to wonder if it was really my calling. The enemy tried to convince me I couldn't speak. My mom and dad always told me that whatever God has for me and my sister, Claire, that he would see us through. They would say, "If it is your true calling, then the desire will never leave you."

I spoke for the first time at the New Year's Eve party for our youth group. The theme for our year is "Shoes off, ready to fight." I have spoken several times since then in Sunday School. In February, we had a youth service on a Wednesday night. All of the young ministers tag teamed. My title was "An Inside Job," it was about matters of the heart. It felt very surreal to stand behind the pulpit for the first time. My life has been blessed to watch my dad, Uncle Scotty, Nana,

Uncle Samuel, and my Papa (Bro. Tim Gordon) preach behind that pulpit. Along with so many others, they have inspired me along the way. I am truly blessed with a wonderful family on both my mom and dad's sides, so much love and such spiritual giants to lead me. Some have gone to make heaven their home, but they left a mark on my life and prayed over me.

My prayer is that everyone reading this will always love the Lord with their whole heart and pursue the calling God has for them.

"...For whither thou goest, I will go; and where thou lodgest, I will lodge: thy people shall be my people, and thy God my God:" Ruth 1:16

The One Who Does the Work Gets the Blessing

By Vicky Keller

Psalm 146:5 Happy is he that hath the God of Jacob for his help, whose hope is in the Lord his God.

Dr. Lavada George began evangelizing full time in 1999. Prior to this she and her husband pastored and had a Christian school. One day in the afternoon, she returned to the school and found the cafeteria had been trashed. She told the Lord, "Why these folks must not want a Christian school, just look at this mess." While standing there, she heard the Lord saying to her. "The one that does the work gets the blessing." Immediately she said, "I'll do the work," then started cleaning up the cafeteria. Sister George told me this story many years ago and it left an impression on me.

1 Thessalonians 5:12 And we beseech you, brethren, to know them which labour among you, and are over you in the Lord, and admonish you;

My family lived in Millington, TN. We started attending church and it was during this time when we received the baptism of the Holy Ghost and we were baptized in Jesus Name. The more we became involved in church and activities we soon discovered how important it was to help in the area of fund raising. Many, many times it was necessary to help our missionaries or raise funds for Tupelo Children's Mansion. We added Sheaves for Christ and Mother's Memorial to the list. The needs were many and the list continued to grow. With this being said, my family was enthusiastically involved and we experienced the joy and blessing that comes with working for the Lord.

After moving to Florence, MS in 1991 the Lord blessed our family with Dr. Jean Holland as our new pastor and all the wonderful saints of Jesus Name Tabernacle. One of the first things I needed to settle was finding employment to support my family. I prayed for direction and felt to go to a temp agency one Friday morning. That afternoon they called and asked me to report to my new job on Tuesday. What was so wonderful about this, it was a State Agency. It was all exciting but it was also a little scary. A new job means opportunities to witness and invite people to church.

After settling into my new job, God started opening the doors for promotions. With my personal life in order I was greatly inspired to become involved in working for the Lord. I love to teach, preach, visit the sick, do Bible studies and you name it I love it. I wanted to work at JNT in some of the ways that I had in Millington. God is so good to his children. He placed the desire in my heart and made the way for me to work for Him. We raised money making and selling peanut brittle, cooking and selling dinners to the public, and yard sales. These efforts made such a difference not only in the financial area, but in the many opportunities to witness. God opened doors for us to invite as many as possible to church.

"Jesus Name Tabernacle" had an annual "Special Service" each year to raise money to help pay the insurance and other costs the church incurred. Pastor Jean Holland asked for those families who could, to donate $100 each year. My method for being prepared for this offering was to save a few dollars each month. God always blessed and I would give my $100 pledge.

Several circumstances happened in my life and the Lord worked it out for me to retire. I continually prayed for the Lord to lead me. My mother and I attended a conference in Arkansas. While at this conference the Lord showed me that things were about to change. I had no idea what kind of change but I was excited and looked forward to what the Lord would do. It was enjoyable to get to see our friends in the ministry. On one occasion I was looking down the hall and out to the parking lot, Sis. George was walking through the door. We began to visit with each other and catching up on all the news was fun. I asked her about her daughters who had traveled with her. She said she didn't have anyone traveling with her at this time. During our conversation, I asked her if it would be possible for me to travel with her. Everything changed instantly. This was a divine appointment. After speaking with Sis. George, I talked with my pastor for confirmation to go and we began an unforgettable journey together reaching for lost souls.

Sis. George was about 70 when we started working in the field together. When she wasn't preaching I would take advantage of that time to travel home. Usually being home anywhere from a few days to a couple of weeks. When she scheduled revivals, I would leave home traveling to her home in Arkansas. Most of the time we would leave the next morning to go where her revival was scheduled. Eventually Sister George wasn't scheduling as many revivals mostly because of her age. My time at home increased so my desire to work for the Lord led me to become more and more involved at JNT, preaching and teaching. But also I wanted to work and help in church fundraising. I love to make peanut brittle so we successfully made and sold it.

In 2012, Pastor Holland had invited some missionaries to come and speak at the church. Not knowing any circumstances pertaining to the church financial situation, we had already scheduled a yard sale at the church the Saturday before they were to be with us. One of the workers who always helps me asked, "How much did I think the sale would bring." "$2000," I said confidently. He looked at me as if to say, "not in this life, time" but never said a word about it to me. All of us worked diligently and at the end of the day we were blessed with over the amount we needed.

I can't even begin to tell you how God went over and above what we asked of Him that day. Our next service (with the missionaries) we had souls receive the Holy Ghost and were baptized in Jesus Name. It was worth every minute of working the yard sale just to see people get their hearts right with God. On another note my friend doesn't ask me any more about the amount we need at our yard sales. I asked him "why." He said laughing, "No need to ask." I've seen God move tremendously every time we step out to work for Him.

We have been here 25 years now. Cannot express in words how much my Pastor, Dr. Jean Holland means to me and my family. She has helped each of us with her King Solomon wisdom. She loves the precious truth and has done everything to promote loving Jesus, loving each other, and being real. "Being Real!" She admonishes us to always be real. What do I think she means by this? Be authentic, sincere, and honest in thoughts and actions. She and Jesus have placed the mantle of Pastor upon Pastor Max Smith. We look forward to following him in the Kingdom in whatever we can be and do.

While traveling evangelizing with Sister George she encouraged me to sing and the words to this song by the Hinsons will forever ring in my heart.

> *Now who can speak to a cripple*
> *And make them stand right up and walk.*
> *And who can cause the deaf and dumb*
> *To hear and start to talk.*
> *Oh and who can calm a fevered brow by just saying let it be.*

With just a little bit of clay touching
Away their blinding eyes can see.

And what could cause an old man that's about to say good-bye
To just lift up both of those dying hands
With a tear running from his eye
With his loved one's gathered all around him
He can smile and say not fear
Cause the one that brought me up
Through the storm will lead me on from here.

I'm telling you he can and to know that he stands
By your side when the world comes crumbling in,
Lord no one's ever done what he had done
He laid down his life but he rose to live again.

In the Beginning

By Dee Wells

Millington, Tennessee, a small town 15 miles north of Memphis, had a large Navy base during the Vietnam War and several years afterwards. My husband was stationed there so our family moved there also. At that time, most of the base operated as a series of schools for the training of Navy airmen after they had completed their basic training. They were trained in various fields associated with the U.S. Navy air wing.

While we were stationed there I was invited to visit the church service at the First United Pentecostal Church. Sister Hazel Simpson was the pastor. I was a Holy Ghost filled conservative Baptist and I was curious about Pentecostal worship. It was different from anything that I was familiar with, however I felt the presence of God like I had never felt it before!

I continued to attend services and heard preaching on baptism in the Name of Jesus, and the oneness of the Godhead. It was an unfamiliar doctrine but it wasn't long until the Holy God of heaven opened my eyes to this truth. All my family and myself were baptized in the Name of Jesus and I witnessed every one of them filled with the Holy Ghost.

Sometime later I began a ministry of feeding the Navy airmen students who attended the church. The mess hall at the base closed Sunday mornings at 11:30 a.m. and did not reopen until Monday morning. The young men were going hungry if they attended church. I began cooking for them on Sunday mornings. The first time I prepared a meal we had eight airmen present. The menu was spaghetti, string beans, rolls, sweet tea, and chocolate cake. Every Sunday after, our group increased. I was privileged to witness these young men return to church and revival began to break out among them. We saw many receive the Holy Ghost and were baptized in Jesus Name. Most of them could stay three or four months, long enough to do basic mentoring. It was an exciting time in my life and I learned to love working for the Lord.

There are always opportunities to work for the Lord if we are willing, and I certainly was. For years, I helped prepare the peanut brittle for fundraising—I popped thousands of pans, which means to slightly flex the metal pan and the candy will pop free. I enjoyed cooking and serving dinners to the public, selling donuts on Saturday mornings to the local businesses, serving pancake breakfasts at the local community center, and oh yes—sold peanut brittle!!

I became the Ladies Auxiliary Leader. It was my responsibility to do fundraising for "Mother's Memorial." The Lord led me to expand the meetings and to invite special speakers. We invited ladies from other churches within our district. It was my privilege again for the Lord to use me to organize and work to prepare programs. Special music and singers would come from other churches. Our ladies provided the refreshments. This became a great outreach for girls and women. Once a year, at the beginning of Christmas season, I invited the ladies and their families and friends to a "Tasting Tea." This served as an outreach for backsliders, family members, and neighbors as well as wonderful fellowship for everyone. The church at Millington continues to do this.

I am deeply grateful for the opportunities the Lord gives us to work in His Kingdom.

Ecclesiastes 3:1 To every thing there is a season, and a time to every purpose under the heaven:

Many years passed and our family experienced a time when we were rather like the children of Israel; wandering in the desert. However, in June of 1991, our precious Lord led us to Florence, MS and Jesus Name Tabernacle We have been so blessed to be a part of this ministry. Our precious Pastor, Dr. Jean Holland, for over twenty-five years, has been everything that we needed. She has led us, guided us, kept us,

encouraged us, and admonished us when we needed it. Pastor Holland had a dream about my family several months after we became a part of JNT. In the dream she was at the church and as she looked toward the entrance of the church a lady entered. She was a rather short elderly lady, and at first Pastor Holland thought she recognized her. The lady continued to walk down the aisle. It was during the church service so she walked over to where our family was sitting. It was our former pastor, Sister Hazel Simpson and she told Pastor Holland, "I've come to see how my people are doing." Pastor Holland realized it was not who she had thought and when she turned the lady disappeared. This was a dream, but it made a lasting impression on each of us. Sister Simpson had passed away but her love and prayers followed us. When Pastor Holland shared this with us, it confirmed that we were exactly where God had led us. Thank you Lord for your tender love, mercy, and compassion for placing us here.

BLOOM WHERE YOU ARE PLANTED

Bobbie Lively

1Corinthians 7:24 Brethren, let every man, wherein he is called, therein abide with God. It was in the winter near the year 2002 when I was privileged to move to Florence, Mississippi. I was blessed with a lovely office and the best church that anyone could ask for.

I was struggling, as we all do, with knowing for sure if I was to continue to be a missionary or travel as an evangelist or just what was I to do. I was in a prayerful frame of mind, and as I looked on the wall near the door there was a plaque that read, "Bloom Where Your Planted."

This was a true message to me that very moment, and I want to share a few short stories that I witnessed at Jesus Name Tabernacle.

Pastor Irma Jean Holland was the most profoundly awesome leader anyone could hope to have. Her singing, preaching, guitar playing, counseling, nurturing, and teaching skills were done with dignity and professional expertise. It was a real joy to observe her on any level of ministry, and the three books of *My Heritage* were designed to share with everyone who will take the time to read them.

By my obedience to bloom where I was obviously being planted afforded me training and opportunities that exceeded my plans. I was asked to help with a minister's class, sponsored to return to Rankin Inlet missions, and encouraged to be a part of outreach in several programs.

What I want to share with you is something that has been mentioned in previous books. This chapter is designed to fill in a few details.

Sister Nancy Howell was the youth minister at that time and her influence flavored everything. Prayer meetings, fundraisers, and the best cook ever.

Her cooking was a ministry. Really!! This brings to mind something that left an impact on me. One afternoon I visited when a lot was going on at church which caused a whole lot of activity for Sister Nancy anyway. Sister Nancy was planning her youth meeting that evening and she was cooking an elaborate meal with all the trimmings.

"Hey, why don't you get a pizza or whatever so you won't be working so hard?" As I blurted this out my eyes met with Sister Nancy's eyes. Her expression was gentle and knowing. What I was unaware of is that she had a love for the members of her class and homemade food and desserts was her expression of just how much they meant to her. Did this matter? It must have, because in the past ten years most of these students are in active ministry.

When she and I first met, she commented that the Lord had sent her someone else to care for. That didn't make sense to me. I could take care of myself, and she was already the busiest person on the planet. As time passed I understood, because I watched her fill every moment with the most perfect servant's heart I had ever witnessed.

JNT is a church and it is a family. Brothers and Sisters in the Lord. Caring and sharing with each other. I witnessed their love for my family and she and Pastor Holland made it possible for me to minister to my family and my personal needs. This could not have happened before the Lord planted me in Florence, Mississippi.

In the early months of 2016, Pastor Holland and Sister Nancy were out and about with the responsibilities concerning the church. But when Pastor called Sister's name, it was with a slurring sound. A stroke was coming on and with tremendous courage and skill on the part of Sister Nancy, they arrived at the hospital. Sister Nancy drove better than any ambulance and with obvious wisdom and courage so as not to waste a minute. She skillfully arranged for everything that would be needed to take the least amount of time. Sister Holland and everyone connected with her was in good hands; Sister Nancy saw to that!!!

The title everyone gives Sister Nancy is "God's Armor Bearer." I personally want to say, and everyone I know agrees, that there is a heart filled with love in this wonderful saint of God.

When Jesus said, John 15:12-13,
This is my commandment, That ye love one another,
as I have loved you. Greater love hath no man than this,
that a man lay down his life for his friends.

Speaking about blooms and plants, it is a sight to behold when you visit their home. Flowers, vegetables, grass trimmed, plants of all sizes and it all blends together in a lovely array. Children, grandchildren, neighbors, and church people love to visit. Oh yes! She decorates her mailbox, too.

The garbage pick-up men always have a special treat when they come by each week. No one is forgotten.

She is a prayer warrior and a Bible scholar. She lives a life of faith, integrity, and diligence. We all need, and are greatly benefited by knowing and working alongside, someone who is committed to the will of God whatever the cost.

Thank you Jesus for planting me in the same garden with Senior Pastor Holland and Sister Nancy Howell.

Pastor Max Smith is married to First Lady Peggy Smith who is Sister Nancy's daughter.

Milton Keynes UK
Ingram Content Group UK Ltd.
UKHW040705050124
435493UK00001B/246